D1398928

Casting Your Cares
Upon the Lord

Kenneth E. Hagin

Unless otherwise indicated, all Scripture quotations in this volume are from the *King James Version* of the Bible.

First Printing 1981

ISBN 0-89276-023-0

In the U.S. write:
Kenneth Hagin Ministries, Inc.
P.O. Box 50126
Tulsa, Oklahoma 74150

In Canada write:
Kenneth Hagin Ministries
P.O. Box 335
Islington (Toronto), Ontario
Canada, M9A 4X3

BOOKS BY KENNETH E. HAGIN

Redeemed From Poverty . . . Sickness . . . Death
What Faith Is
Seven Vital Steps To Receiving the Holy Spirit
Right and Wrong Thinking
Prayer Secrets
Authority of the Believer
How To Turn Your Faith Loose
The Key to Scriptural Healing
The Ministry of a Prophet
The Origin and Operation of Demons
Demons and How To Deal With Them
Ministering to the Oppressed
Praying To Get Results
The Present Day Ministry of Jesus Christ
The Gift of Prophecy
Healing Belongs to Us
The Real Faith
The Interceding Christian
How You Can Know the Will of God
Man on Three Dimensions
The Human Spirit
Turning Hopeless Situations Around
Faith Food for Autumn
Faith Food for Winter
Faith Food for Spring
Faith Food for Summer
The New Birth
Why Tongues?
In Him
God's Medicine
You Can Have What You Say
How To Write Your Own Ticket With God
Don't Blame God
Words
Plead Your Case
How To Keep Your Healing
Laying on of Hands
A Better Covenant

Having Faith in Your Faith
Five Hindrances to Growth in Grace
Why Do People Fall Under the Power?
The Bible Way To Receive the Holy Spirit
I Believe in Visions
Exceedingly Growing Faith
The Woman Question
New Thresholds of Faith
Prevailing Prayer to Peace
Concerning Spiritual Gifts
Bible Faith Study Course
Bible Prayer Study Course
The Holy Spirit and His Gifts
Growing Up, Spiritually
Redimido De La Pobreza, La Enfermedad, La Muerte
La Fe, Lo Que Es
Siete Pasos Para Recibir El Espiritu Santo
?Piensa Usted Bien? O Mal?
La Autoridad Del Creyente
Como Desatar Su Fe
Seven Things You Should Know About Divine Healing
El Shaddai
Zoe: The God-Kind of Life
A Commonsense Guide to Fasting
How You Can Be Led By The Spirit of God
What To Do When Faith Seems Weak and Victory Lost
The Name of Jesus
The Art of Intercession

BOOKS BY KENNETH HAGIN JR.

Man's Impossibility—God's Possibility
Because of Jesus
Unity: Key to the Age of Power
Faith Worketh by Love
Blueprint for Building Strong Faith
Seven Hindrances to Healing
The Past Tense of God's Word
Healing: A Forever-Settled Subject
How To Make the Dream God Gave You Come True

Contents

Chapter 1
The Prayer of Commitment

Ephesians 6:18 — a Scripture written to the Church —
is one of my favorite verses on the subject of prayer.

EPHESIANS 6:18
**18 Praying always with all prayer and supplication in
the Spirit, and watching thereunto with all persever-
ance and supplication for all saints.**

Another translation says "all manner of prayer." Yet
another says "all kinds of prayer." We need all kinds of
prayer — not just one kind. The Bible speaks of several
kinds of prayer.

One is "the prayer of commitment," or casting your
cares upon the Lord. Our main text on this is First Peter
5:7, *"Casting all your care upon him; for he careth for you."*
That's from the *King James Version.*

My favorite translation of this particular verse is from
The Amplified Bible: "Casting the whole of your care — all
your anxieties, all your worries, all your concerns, once
and for all — on Him; for He cares for you affectionately,
and cares about you watchfully."

Philippians 4:6 contains instructions concerning
prayer given by the Spirit of God through the Apostle
Paul. The *King James Version* reads, *"Be careful for
nothing; but in every thing by prayer and supplication with
thanksgiving let your requests be made known unto God."*

That phrase "Be careful for nothing" is unclear to us in
the 20th century. A modern translation reads, "Do not
have any anxiety about anything." Another translation,
which I like better, says, "Do not fret or have any anxiety
about anything, but in everything by prayer and supplica-

tion with thanksgiving let your requests be made known unto God."

Now turn back to the sixth chapter of Matthew's Gospel.

> **MATTHEW 6:25-34**
> 25 Therefore I say unto you, Take no thought for your life, what ye shall eat, or what ye shall drink; nor yet for your body, what ye shall put on. Is not the life more than meat, and the body than raiment?
> 26 Behold the fowls of the air: for they sow not, neither do they reap, nor gather into barns; yet your heavenly Father feedeth them. Are ye not much better than they?
> 27 Which of you by taking thought can add one cubit unto his stature?
> 28 And why take ye thought for raiment? Consider the lilies of the field, how they grow; they toil not, neither do they spin:
> 29 And yet I say unto you, That even Solomon in all his glory was not arrayed like one of these.
> 30 Wherefore, if God so clothe the grass of the field, which to day is, and to morrow is cast into the oven, shall he not much more clothe you, O ye of little faith?
> 31 Therefore take no thought, saying, What shall we eat? or, What shall we drink? or, Wherewithal shall we be clothed?
> 32 (For after all these things do the Gentiles seek:) for your heavenly Father knoweth that ye have need of all these things.
> 33 But seek ye first the kingdom of God, and his righteousness; and all these things shall be added unto you.
> 34 Take therefore no thought for the morrow: for the morrow shall take thought for the things of itself. Sufficient unto the day is the evil thereof.

Different rules regulate different kinds of prayer. If you take the rules that regulate one kind of prayer and try to apply them to another, it will lead to confusion. There-fore, we need to learn which kind of prayer we need to do under certain circumstances and conditions.

In crusades and meetings around the country we endeavor to move people to faith — to believe God now — to get an answer now. We're only in their areas for a brief time; we're usually not holding prayer seminars. In order to help the most people we possibly can, we try to move them to believe God to receive for their own individual needs; primarily in the healing area.

But that brief instruction we give is not the last word on the subject of faith and prayer. And if people accept it as being the last word, they will be disillusioned in life.

Because we emphasize the prayer of faith, some people have faith in my faith and they don't have faith in their own faith. They want me to pray the prayer of faith for them. They come up to me with prayer requests. Of course the Bible does teach us to pray for one another, and the Bible does teach intercession, but we need to determine which kind of prayer will work for a given condition.

One day after a service, a woman came up to me and said, "Brother Hagin, I want you to pray for me."

I said, "What for?"

She looked surprised and said, "Do I have to tell you?"

I said, "Well, I'm not going to pray unless you do tell me, because I wouldn't know what we're praying about otherwise. I can't believe for something I don't know about, and I can't agree on something unless I know what I'm agreeing on. What is your request?"

She began to cry. She said, "Brother Hagin, the burdens of life — the cares, the worries of life — are just so heavy I can't bear them. I wanted you to pray that the Lord would do one of two things: He'd either take about half of them away, because I can carry half of them — I just can't carry all of them — or else He would give me grace to carry them."

My heart went out to her. I did my best to help her. I said, "Sister, I can't pray either way. That would be unscriptural. You see, the prayer of faith will not work in that case. In fact, there is only one kind of prayer that will work in this case: the prayer of commitment. Isn't it wonderful, Sister, that you and I already have the answer?"

She looked startled.

I said, "We have inside information on the subject." (What I meant was inside-the-Bible information.)

I said, "You see, the Word of God tells us exactly what to do with our worries, our concerns, our anxieties."

I quoted to her from the *King James Version* first. I said, "In First Peter 5:7, the Holy Spirit said through the Apostle Paul, *'Casting all your care upon him; for he careth for you.'* And *The Amplified Bible* says, 'Casting the whole of your care — all your anxieties, all your worries, all your concerns, once and for all — on Him; for He cares for you affectionately, and cares about you watchfully.' "

I told her, "You don't have to do it every day. You do it once and for all. From then on, you're carefree."

She looked up at me and said, "You're hard-hearted. You're just hard-hearted!"

I put all the kindness in my voice I could, and I said, "Dear Sister, I'm not hard-hearted. I didn't write the Bible! I wasn't the One who said that. That's God's Word, and God loves you."

"Yeah," she replied, *"but you don't know what I've got to*

worry about!"

I said, "Dear Sister, I'm sure I don't know what you've got to worry about, but God knows — He knows everything — and it's God's Word that says, 'Casting the whole of your care — all your anxieties, all your worries, all your concerns, once and for all — on Him.'"

She said, "I just can't do it."

I said, "Yes you can. God is just and kind and good, and He didn't ask you to do something you can't do."

It seemed to me that anybody would be glad to find that verse in the Bible and would be thrilled to act upon it. But she turned, walked away, and said, "I couldn't give up worrying."

Chapter 2
The Sin of Worry

The only sin that I had a great problem to get rid of was the sin of worry. (That statement always goes over big because most people still have that sin, and they don't want to acknowledge that it's wrong.)

I never had any trouble with lying. After I got born again, I never wanted to lie anymore. I haven't had any problem with that one at all. And I never had any problem with other sins. No, the toughest time I had was with this worry business.

You know my story. I was born again on the 22nd day of April 1933 at 20 minutes till 8 o'clock on Saturday night in the south bedroom of 405 North College Street in the city of McKinney, Texas.

I never had a normal childhood. I had become bedfast. I'd gone to Baptist Sunday School and church all my life, so I had a Bible. I had read so many chapters each week just so I could say I had read them — but they didn't mean anything to me. I didn't think you were *supposed* to understand the Bible.

But the morning after I became born again, I asked my family to bring me the Bible. I got blessed just looking at the cover, where it said "Holy Bible." Then I looked inside. I got blessed just reading the table of contents. Oh, when you're born again, the whole thing becomes alive and new to you!

In Vacation Bible School, we had learned to sing the books of the Bible, and we could rattle them off with head knowledge, but it didn't mean a thing to us. Now I was born again. I read the names of the Old and New Testament books. Blessed be God, when you begin to say them out of your spirit, they mean something. I got blessed just reading the books of the Bible.

The doctor had recently warned me, "You could go at any minute," so I thought, *I'll start in the New Testament since my time is limited. I am going to get in here in a hurry and find out what belongs to me.*

I opened to Matthew. Then I prayed, "Lord, before I ever start reading, I promise You this: I make this covenant with You. I'll never doubt anything that I read in your Word. And the moment I read it and understand it, I'll put it into practice."

I got as far as Matthew 6 and read that 34th verse. *"Take therefore no thought for the morrow: for the morrow shall take thought for the things of itself. Sufficient unto the day is the evil thereof."*

I was reading out of a New Testament, because it was lighter and easier for me to hold. It had a little footnote at the bottom of the page. It referred me to Philippians 4:6: *"Be careful for nothing; but in every thing by prayer and supplication with thanksgiving let your requests be made known unto God."*

It also referred me to First Peter 5:7: *"Casting all your care upon him; for he careth for you."* Then whoever wrote the footnotes said, "God doesn't want you to worry or be anxious about anything."

I was just a youngster — just 15 years old (this was a little before my 16th birthday). You talk about *worrying* — I was taught to worry from the time I was a little child. I was actually a "worrywart." Do you know what a "worry-wart" is? I was one of them.

My mother and grandmother were *world champion worriers,* and I had learned to worry from them.

When I first became bedfast, I had two doctors. Finally there were five doctors on my case. They didn't tell me much about what was wrong with me. When you're an invalid, you can lie there and imagine that everything in the world is wrong with you. And you're sure taking thought about tomorrow, because you may not even be here tomorrow!

But I had just promised God, "I'll practice whatever I understand in your Word." The Bible had been all light, joy, and a blessing to me. But the further I got into Matthew, it became dark, with no joy, no blessing, no reality to it. I stopped to check up. I asked myself, *What's wrong here?*

Matthew 6 kept popping up. "You said you'd put into practice whatever you read and understood."

"Dear Lord," I said, "if a person's got to live like Matthew 6 said, I'll never make it. I can't live without worrying. That's as much a part of me as my hands and feet!"

I went on reading, but I never got a thing out of it. That was the 23rd day of April 1933, and it took me until July 4th to get out of the sixth chapter of Matthew.

There's no use in continuing to read the Bible if it is not a joy and a thrill to your spirit. You need to go back to where you quit walking in the light, start walking in the light, and it will be light again to you. (And you know where it was you quit.)

Somebody will say, "No, I don't."

Now quit lying about it. Repent for lying first of all. I know you know, because I was just like you. I tried to make excuses for myself, but the Lord didn't listen to me, so I had to go back to the sixth chapter of Matthew again and get on the right track. Then the Bible became all light to me again.

I never will forget July 4, 1933. I had a pity party all day. I cried all day long. I was sure I couldn't do what Matthew 6 said.

"Lord," I complained, "if we've got to live like that — if we've got to live without worrying — I might as well give up now. I'll never make it as a Christian!"

I was feeling sorry for myself. I couldn't live like the Bible said to live, and besides that, I was dying. And I wanted to blame it all on God.

I said, "Lord, You haven't done right by me! Here I am just 15 years old, and I've got to die — the doctor said so. You know I've been physically handicapped all of my life. I was born prematurely with a deformed heart."

Then I said, "Look at So-and-so. (I named a certain boy who started school with me in the first grade. He lived a few blocks away.) He's wearing good clothes. He's got money in his pocket. He's got his health — and I know how he got his money.

"They're not supposed to do it — it's illegal — but they gamble in the back of the drugstore. He entices others in there. He is just a teenager — that's illegal, too — but they'd just as soon take a teenager's money as an adult's. No matter what he wins, he gives all the money back because he's working for them. And the other boys lose all their money, You know. He's a 'shill,' as they call them. So, he's got money; he's got clothes; he's got health — *and I never was as mean as him!*

"You know, Lord, I've always been pretty good. Of course, handicapped like I was, I couldn't do too much that was wrong . . . *But I never was as bad as him!*"

Then I said, "There is So-and-so (and I named a boy who lived in my end of town and who started school with me in the first grade). He's got money. He's got new clothes. *He even has an automobile!*" (For a teenager to have an automobile in 1933 — brother! They were fortunate to have a bicycle in those Depression days.)

"And he's running around in an almost-new automobile — and I know how he got his money! His brother is a bootlegger, and he runs it for him in his car. *And I never was as mean as him!*"

I was telling the Lord about these other people, pointing out to Him that I wasn't bootlegging, I wasn't gambling, "And You know," I told Him, "I never was as bad as either of those fellows. And I don't have any good clothes. And I don't have any health. And I have to die. And You've been better to them — *as mean as they are* — than You have been to me. Poor ol' me!" And I began crying even harder.

I continued, "And now I've gotten saved — born again — and I've got to quit worrying, and I know that I can't."

I was about dead to begin with, but I was about to worry myself to death trying to figure out what was wrong with me. You imagine you have every disease in the world. (Thank God for Dr. Robason, one of my doctors. He finally came and sat by my bed about a month later and told me exactly what was wrong with me physically.)

If I were preaching here against using tobacco, a lot of people would jump up and down and shout, "Praise God, that's right, brother — preach it!" But the sin of worry is worse than the sin of tobacco. God doesn't want you to be bound by *any* habit, but the habit of worry is worse than the tobacco habit!

Doctors have told me that there are more people sick in hospitals, mental institutions — and already dead — because of worry than any other cause. Worry will kill you. (Tobacco will just half kill you, and you'll stink while you're dying. But worry will kill you.)

Once you start preaching like this on people's pet habit, they'll start to feel sorry for themselves. They think God is not treating them right; the preacher is not treating them right; the world is not treating them right; their brother is not treating them right; and nothing is right. So they have themselves a pity party, like I did. What a struggle I had that July Fourth 1933. At 6 p.m., Momma was by my bed again, trying to comfort me.

I said, "Momma, if you just *want* to live, will that help any? I mean — just *want* to live?"

She said, "Well, that's about 50 percent of the battle."

I made a little adjustment on the inside of me, and I said, "Well, I've got 50 percent of it made now. I'll lay that aside and go to work on the other 50 percent."

The minute I said that, something on the inside of me said, "Matthew 6." I knew what He meant.

I turned back to Matthew 6 and read it. After I finished the 34th verse, I said, "All right, Lord. Forgive me. I repent. I repent for worrying. And I promise You this day I'll never worry again the longest day I live. I promise You this day I'll never be discouraged again. I promise You this day I'll never have the blues again."

Thank God I haven't — and I've passed up some marvelous opportunities, too!

I started practicing that as a teenager. It's easier if you start early in life; it's more difficult when you're older, because you've been going a certain way for many years.

It's easier for me now. At first it was difficult, but I refused to worry.

I didn't know about divine healing then — I hadn't gotten far enough in the Bible; I hadn't gotten over to Mark 11:23,24 yet, so I really didn't know that I could be healed.

I still had my physical condition. It still looked like I was going to die. Not only was I bedfast, but every day I would have three to five heart seizures or heart attacks. My heart would stop and I'd think it was never going to start again. I'd fight to stay alive with every fiber in my being. I wore all the varnish off of my bed, right down to the bare wood, just holding on. You hold on with everything you've got to stay here.

Right in the middle of one of those attacks, I turned loose. I turned everything over to the Lord, fell back on my pillow, and said, "Let 'er go. I know where I'm going, anyhow." I never had any more problems with fear. I still had the attacks, but they didn't bother me. I had cast that care upon the Lord.

So I started living that way. I never read a book on the subject; I just saw it in the Bible.

Chapter 3
'Not Enough Sense To Worry'

When you walk by faith — when you do what the Bible says — you're an oddity to others, even in the church world. They think something is wrong with you because you don't worry.

After I was healed, I started praying for the sick. I anointed folks with oil. That didn't go over too well with the Baptists.

I was never an ordained Baptist preacher, although they offered to ordain me. They can ordain you in the local church. In fact, the pastor said, "We'll ordain you, Kenneth, on one condition: if you'll tone down just a little bit on this healing business. Go ahead and preach a little prayer and faith if you want to, but just tone down on this healing business."

I said, "I was planning on toning *up* on it!"

I didn't pray for anybody publicly back then. I'd preach it publicly, but would pray for them privately, and I was planning to start praying publicly for them. That's the reason I said, "I was planning on toning up on it."

I never will forget it. When I told the pastor that, he said, "Well, just forget it, then. Just forget it," and walked off and left me. And I don't remember ever seeing him again. Then, of course, when I got the baptism of the Holy Spirit and spoke with other tongues, I did get "the left foot of fellowship" sure enough.

I came over among the Full Gospel people. They had the baptism of the Holy Spirit — they spoke with other tongues — and I was sure they were all sprouting wings. It took me a little while to find out that those weren't wings they were sprouting; those were just their shoulder blades sticking out!

I took a Full Gospel church to pastor, and being new in Full Gospel circles, I didn't know that nobody else would pastor this church. It was a "trouble" church. But God told me to take it. I guess the reason was because He knew I wouldn't worry about it.

In those days, it was a common practice to have a pastors' fellowship meeting the first Monday of every month. I'd go and find all the pastors lined up, talking. They'd say to me, "How goes the battle?"

I'd walk by them and say, "Men, I don't have a care." They'd stand there and blink their eyes. They'd say to one another, "I don't believe he's got enough sense to worry!"

One of my neighboring pastors told them, "I know he does have a care. He's got the hardest church to pastor there is in this section. He's got this problem and that problem." (He knew more about my church problems than I did!)

I'd get up to preach on Sunday mornings and be tempted to yield to the flesh. I felt like starting in with the deacon board, taking them one by one, skinning them, salting their hides, and hanging them up on a wall of the church; then starting in with the Sunday School superintendent and all of the Sunday School teachers, skinning them, salting their hides, and hanging them up on the other wall of the church.

But when I had that kind of temptation, I'd turn to the 13th chapter of First Corinthians and preach on love, or I'd turn to Revelation 21 and 22 and preach on heaven.

The first year I pastored that church, I spent most of my time preaching on love and heaven! It's amazing what preaching on love and heaven will do. When you can get everybody loving one another and heading to heaven, things straighten out pretty well!

I said, "Lord, I know something ought to be said, but I don't know what to say. And I know something ought to be done, but I don't know what to do. I'm just a novice when it comes to pastoring. I'm going to do right. I'm going to preach the Word. I'm going to treat everybody the same. I'm going to visit the sick — and I'm going to turn all the rest of it over to You, because this is my care, and You said to cast our care upon You."

It was amazing what happened when I turned it over to Him. We had constant revival! I mean, every week! Every weekend we had people saved, baptized with the Holy Spirit, and healed. And God blessed us so that when I left that church, 40 preachers put in their application for it. (When I took it, nobody would have it.)

It wasn't what I did; I cast all of my care upon Him. But that doesn't mean I didn't do my part. I studied, I prepared messages, etc. But the worry part — the anxiety part of it — I turned over to the Lord. I didn't carry it.

The parsonage was right next door to the church, and some of the people would stop by and tell me things. I would reply, "I'm not going to worry about it. I'll tell you the truth: If the church catches fire and burns down and it's nighttime and I'm asleep, don't even wake me. Just let it burn. We'll just build a bigger church.

"If the deacon board gets in a fist fight in the front yard of the church, don't come over to the parsonage and disturb me. Just let them fight it out. After they get through, I'll pray them through and get them right with God. I'm not going to lose a wink of sleep. I'm not going to miss a meal about this. (I did fast if the Lord led me.) I've turned it over to the Lord."

If you don't commit your cares and anxieties to the Lord, there will come a time when all of your prayers, and all the prayers of the church, radio and TV ministers, and everybody else you can get to pray will be to no avail. When they all get through, you're going to be right where you were when you started as long as you hold on to those things yourself. You're going to have to turn them over to the Lord.

Every one of the preachers who made fun of me eventually came to me and said, "You've got the answer. We don't. Our wives have had nervous breakdowns. Your wife hasn't. We had to retire from the ministry or take a year or two off to rest. You just keep going."

One fellow who was only 39 years old wasn't feeling well physically. Finally his wife said to him, "I believe you owe it to me and our daughter to go to a doctor and at least find out what's wrong with you." (In those days, Pentecostal preachers believed solely in trusting God and not going to doctors.)

So he went to the doctor. After checking him, the doctor said, "Well, there isn't anything wrong with you as far as sickness and disease are concerned, but you've worn yourself out. You're only 39 years old, but you've got the body of a 90-year-old man." (A 90-year-old man hasn't got much longer to live, friends!)

"I'll tell you what you've done," the doctor continued. "You've carried the load of everybody in the church — all their burdens — all their worries. You've eaten these problems at meal time. You've slept with these problems. You've talked about them. You've carried them."

"Yes, that's what I've done," the pastor agreed.

"Well," the doctor said, "you might live another couple of years if you give up the ministry and rest."

Thank God I came along to hold him a meeting, taught him how to trust God, and got him healed. I read years later in a denominational magazine that he retired from pastoring at age 75, but was still preaching. Glory! When he was 39, the doctor said he was going to die.

I learned to walk in the strength of the Lord and cast my cares on Him.

"Casting the whole of your care — all your anxieties, all your worries, all your concerns, *once and for all* — on Him; for He cares for you affectionately, and cares about you watchfully," *The Amplified Bible* renders that Scripture.

When you turn it over to Him, you don't have it anymore. He's got it. Then you can say, "I'm carefree," even when it's still there from the natural standpoint. Because you're not carrying that load; He is.

We used to sing a song that went, "Take your burden to the Lord and leave it there." The trouble with most people is that they come to the altar, or wherever they pray, take their burdens to the Lord all right, tell Him about them — and then when they get up from that place of prayer, they pick their burdens up again!

It helps to imagine your burdens as a 100-pound sack. People put it on their backs and carry it home with them from their place of prayer. No! Leave it there! Leave it there! "Casting the whole of your care ... ONCE AND FOR ALL on Him," that verse says. So I refuse to worry. (Of course, when you don't, you're an oddity.)

Once I was fumbling around with the key, trying to get the parsonage door open, and holding our son Ken in my arms at the same time. My wife was holding Patsy, who was just a baby. (Ken was bigger and heavier.)

Oretha said, "I don't believe you would worry if both the kids and I fell dead right here on the front porch."

I said, "Well, I'd be a fool to start worrying then, wouldn't I? That would be stupid." (The Lord plainly said, "Which of you by taking thought can add one cubit unto his stature," Matt. 6:27.) I would have been concerned, but I wouldn't have worried about it.

Oretha finally learned not to worry. I heard her say to another preacher's wife one time, "Well, I finally learned it works. I don't ever worry." And right at that time in our life, you talk about having problems and needs! They were piled on us knee deep. But she wasn't worrying, because she had learned to cast those cares upon the Lord.

We can do it — we can cast all of our cares on Him — because He said to do it. He's not unjust. He's not going to tell you or me to do something we can't do. That would be unjust.

Chapter 4
Dealing With Anxieties

It's easy to find out why prayer doesn't work all the time for some people. They want you to pray the prayer of faith and get the victory for them — but they want to hold onto their cares, too.

Did you notice that verse in Philippians 4? Let's look at it again. Here is instruction. Why not take God's instruction on prayer? Don't you believe God knows what He is talking about?

> **PHILIPPIANS 4:6**
> 6 **BE CAREFUL FOR NOTHING;** but in every thing by prayer and supplication with thanksgiving let your requests be made known unto God.

That's from the *King James Version*. We don't talk that way today. Today we would say, "In nothing be anxious," or "Do not fret or have any anxiety about anything."

Notice that this is instruction about prayer. What is the first thing the Lord said to do? Deal with your anxieties; deal with your worries. That's the first thing. And that's the first thing the Lord dealt with me about. I didn't know as much about the Bible then, but the Spirit of God led me in line with the Word.

So do that first. Then pray.

It's easy enough to practice the second part of the verse (*"in every thing by prayer and supplication with thanksgiving let your requests be made known unto God"*), but this part is not going to work without taking the first step (*"Be careful for nothing"*).

Do you understand? The first thing the Lord said was, "Do not fret or have any anxiety about anything." Take that step first.

When you give people the Word of God, some accuse you of being hard-hearted. Wanting to help people is not being hard-hearted, however.

I was holding a meeting in South Texas once, and a Full Gospel minister contacted me through the pastor to see if I would talk to him. He was in a lot of trouble. I knew him, so I said, "Tell him to come here. I will talk to him."

So he came to that town and he told me his problems. Among other things, he was being sued, and that was going to cost him a lot of money in lawyers' fees alone. Troubles were piled on him. He was so nervous, he hadn't eaten for days. His stomach was jumping because he was worried, fretful, and full of anxiety. He couldn't even keep water on his stomach. He couldn't sleep at night. He was full of anxiety with all of this staring him in the face.

He wanted me to pray the prayer of faith that would straighten out all of his problems.

I realized I had to deal with his anxieties before I could get the prayer to work, so I began to talk to him along these lines. I even gave him the same Scriptures I've been giving you, encouraging him to cast all of his care, anxieties, worries, and concerns on the Lord before taking his problems to the Lord in prayer.

He said, "Why won't the Lord hear me? I've prayed, and prayed, and prayed. I've done everything I know to do, and I can't find any relief." He was full of anxiety and fear, that's why.

I began to tell him what the Bible says. And this born-again, Spirit-filled, tongue-talking, Bible-believing, divine healing-believing, miracle-believing, Full Gospel minister said to me, "Well, everybody doesn't have as much faith as you do."

I said, "It isn't a matter of faith, dear Brother. You've got the same Bible I've got. I'm not telling you to do something I haven't done. I don't like to magnify your problem, but let me tell you about a few problems I've faced . . . ." And I told him — and they were worse than what he was facing.

He began to soften. He asked, "What did you do?" (He saw I had been about 10 times worse off than he thought he was.)

I replied, "I never missed a meal. I never missed a wink of sleep. I'll tell you what I did . . . ." *The Amplified Bible* had been published by then, so I read these verses to him out of it.

I told him, "I got down by my bed and read these verses to the Lord. I said to Him, 'See, You told me right here, "Do not fret or have any anxiety about anything," and I'm not going to do it. I'm going to do what You told me to do. You said, "In every thing by prayer and supplication with thanksgiving let your requests be made known," so I'm bringing this problem to You and turning it over to You. Now I'm going to thank You for the answer and go to bed. *Now You've got it. You work on it while I'm asleep.'*"

"Do you mean that it worked that easy for you?" the preacher said.

"No," I said. "I didn't say it was easy. I'd wake up in the middle of the night at first, and that problem would hit me. I'd start thinking about it. I couldn't go back to sleep, so I got out of bed, got on my knees, opened my Bible, and read it to the Lord and to myself.

"I'd say, 'There it is, Lord. I'm not going to take it back. The devil is trying to bring it back to me. He brought a picture of it to me, but it's your problem. You keep working on it. I'm going back to sleep now.' "

I said to the preacher, "I had a little struggle there for a day or two, but I got it over into His hands, I rested, and He worked it all out."

Then this preacher asked — and you'd think he would know the Bible works, for he was Full Gospel — "Will that work for me?"

I said, "Certainly it'll work for you."

"All right," he said. "I'll do it. I'll do it myself."

I said, "I'll agree with you. Go on home and do it."

I saw him afterwards, and he admitted, "Oh, I had a struggle. I couldn't sleep. But I got out of bed three times, read those verses you gave me — I knew they were in the Bible, but I had never acted on them in my life — and I said, 'Lord, it's yours and I'm going to turn it over to You.' And I finally went to sleep.

"The next night," he said, "it was a little easier. By the third night it was a breeze, and after that night I could eat, sleep, and my stomach didn't jump anymore. Then after about 10 days, they contacted me about the lawsuit and said, 'The suit has been dropped. Things have been taken care of. Everything is fine.' I thought, *Dear God! That lawsuit nearly killed me, but as soon as I got it into your hands, You worked it out in just a few days*. Hallelujah!"

Say this out loud: "He is our burden-bearer."

Now make it personal: "He is *my* burden-bearer. He knows all about me. He carries the load. I turn it over to Him. Hallelujah!"

Several years ago we were building on four buildings at once at RHEMA Bible Training Center in Tulsa. That takes a lot of cash flow. We were in financial difficulty.

There would be every reason in the world to worry at a time like that. Some of the people may have, but I refused to.

A minister friend and his wife came here to visit. We were driving them around the campus showing them what we were building, and I remember he said to me, "Ohhh, Brother! Ohhh! I know you must carry a *heavy load!*"

"No," I said. "I don't carry any load at all. I'm carefree, load-free, anxiety-free, worry-free, and burden-free, hallelujah!"

I didn't tell him anything about the struggle we were in right then; I never even mentioned it to him. Why? Because I had already turned it over to the Lord. The Lord had it, and He was working on it.

Instead, I told the minister, "To tell you the real truth about the matter, it wouldn't bother me at all to close this thing down; I didn't want to do it to begin with. I didn't want a school. I was enjoying it out there in field ministry, going from crusade to crusade, seminar to seminar. I was having a high time, and the Lord came along and disturbed me. I never wanted to build any training center. I didn't want one. But the Lord said, 'Do it.'

"I'll tell you exactly what I said to the Lord. I speak very plainly to Him. I don't talk in 'religious' terms to God. I figure He knows us anyway. I just talk to Him plain, for He's my Father.

"I said to Him, 'Lord, I didn't want to build this school anyway. It wasn't my plan or my idea. I didn't want to do it, and I still don't want to, but You said to do it. We've done what You said to do, and I'm going to turn it over to You.

" 'It won't bother me — I won't be the least bit embarrassed at all — if we close it up. It won't embarrass me. I'm not embarrassed. I've turned it over to You. If it doesn't succeed, do You know what I'm going to do? I'm going all over the United States and tell on You. I'm going to tell them You weren't big enough to put it over.

" 'So there it is. You've got it. I'm not going to miss a meal; I'm not going to lose a wink of sleep.' "

And I told the minister, "I slept well every night, and I ate well every day while He worked on the project. Some way or other He managed to put it over! You can see that!"

Chapter 5
Turn Loose of Your Problem

You're going to get into difficulties in life. You're not going to float through life on flowery beds of ease. The crises of life come to all of us. *The difference is if we know the Word;* if we know the Spirit of God; if we know how to pray correctly.

Some of you are holding onto cares and anxieties. You're still fretting. In fact, you've even gone beyond fretting. You're "stewing." And others are possibly boiling over with anxiety, care, and concern.

What God wants you to do is turn it over to Him. No, I didn't say it was easy; especially if you've been in the habit of worry for a long time. *Get in the habit of faith instead.* Just release the worry habit into His hands.

Say, "Lord, I'm putting it into your hands. I'm going to turn that over to You. I refuse to fret anymore, I refuse to worry anymore. I refuse to be unduly concerned anymore about this. I refuse to be full of care. You said to cast it *all* on You because You love me; You care for me affectionately and You care about me watchfully, and I thank You for it.

"It's in your hands, Lord. It's in your hands from this moment on. I rest on You. Thank You, Master."

Yes, the devil will bring a picture of it back to your mind after you get into bed tonight. What are you going to do? Start laughing at him!

Say, "Yes, devil, you brought that picture back, but I'm not worried about it. I turned that over to the Lord. And while I'm asleep, He's working on the case, ha, ha." And then go to sleep. That is being a doer of the Word and not a hearer only (James 1:22).

There are those who are on the verge of receiving their manifestation for healing, but it hasn't come yet — and the reason is because you are holding onto that sickness, disease, or physical condition. Turn it loose! TURN IT LOOSE! Quit holding onto it. Let it go, and just lean back on Jesus. Just fall back on Him. Jesus is there. Say it out loud: "Jesus is there."

Our text says, "He cares for you affectionately." You see, He likes you. Yes, He really does. Yes, He does. Even *you*. He likes you. He loves you. He cares for you affectionately and cares about you watchfully."

He is watching. He'll see you. Just turn loose and fall back into His arms. Glory to God, He'll catch you.

Just relax and rest in Him, and you'll find that your symptoms will disappear.

Prophecy

You see, the Word of God does not just work for one,
And it is not written just for the benefit of one;
But the Word of God belongs unto ALL.
Take the Word as a special message from the kind, loving,
*　giving heart;*
From your own Father,
And apply it unto yourself.
Act upon it with the simplicity of a little child,
And you'll get results every time.